a Pocket Bible St

Mean

Hayley DiMarco

Hungry
Planet

R
Revell
a division of Baker Publishing Group
Grand Rapids, Michigan

Published by Revell
a division of Baker Publishing Group
P.O. Box 6287, Grand Rapids, MI 49516-6287
www.revellbooks.com

Printed in the United States of America

ISBN 978-0-8007-3221-9 (pbk.)

Creative direction: Hungry Planet
Interior design: Sarah Lowrey Brammeier

Contents

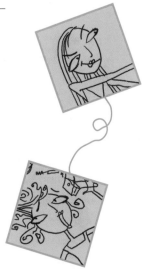

How to Use

It's PB&J time. Time to feast on the hearty protein of God's Word mixed with the sweet goodness of grace. Let the truth stick to the roof of your mouth and satisfy your hunger. This study will offer a full meal for you on the subject of mean girls. With it you can expect to learn all about the subject of mean, why people are mean, how you can change mean, and how to deal when mean won't change. If you have a problem with mean in your life, then this study will help you to easily and quickly digest the Word of God to allow it to nourish your soul and heal your hurts at the hands of mean. It's a guided tour of God's Word, filled with helpful suggestions and truths as well as thought-provoking and self-exploring questions.

This Book

You can do this study by yourself or in a group, but in a group or with a partner is ideal (more on that in a minute). And you can peer lead or find an adult to do it with you. Just go online at www.hungryplanet.net and download the leader's guide of your choice and you are off and running!

So here you have it, a study for girls who are done with mean and want God's help in getting free from it. Whether or not you've read *Mean Girls: Facing Your Beauty Turned Beast,* this study will add to your understanding of God's thoughts on the subject of mean.

Before we start, though, let's lay out a few guidelines that will help you make the most of your study.

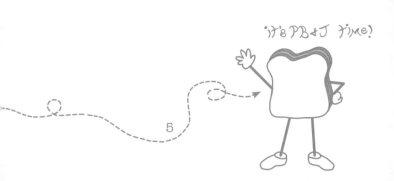

it's PB&J time!

What's up ladies?

Your Girl Crew

First, let me just say that I hope you are doing this book with at least one other girl. In order for us to change the face of girldom, we're going to have to have groups of girls working together to fight off mean. And besides, it will be better for you to have other girls to work through this with. Maybe you've been a meany in the past and you want to stop all that nonsense, or maybe you've been mean but you feel justified. Either way, it would be good to have someone to hear you out and tell if you're crazy or not (I mean, someone besides me). So if you don't have a friend or a group of friends reading a book just like this right now and meeting with you at least once a week to talk about it, then run, don't walk, to the nearest phone

Make a list!
Who's in your crew?

and call a friend. Get the girls in your youth group to get a book of their own, talk to your youth pastor, whatever it takes—just get someone who will go through this journey with you.

So I hope you enjoy! Now sit down and take a bite of your PB&J!

Note for Group Leaders:

Hey, check out the leader's guides on our website. There are two: one for you if you want to lead a group of your friends, and one if you have an adult leading the group. The guide will help you answer the hard questions and keep your group on task. So check out hungryplanet.net or nomoremean.com and download that guide today!

1

Week One

My Mean,
Your Mean,
Our Mean—
What Do You
Mean?

Jesus said that in this world you will have trouble, and I think that mean girls have made that their mission.

"In this world I will fulfill Jesus' promise for you and give you trouble." How kind of them. Ugh! Mean girls, they can really make a mess of your life, but you need to know that you aren't alone. Girls all over the world suffer from, well, other girls. It's almost expected—if you are a girl, then there is going to be another girl who hates you. But does it have to be that way, or is there something we can do?

My Mean

Growing up I was hounded by Mean Girls. I went to a small school, and it seemed like all but two of the girls hated me. Mean Girls plotted against me, laughed at me, lied about me, and did all they could to make me hate my life. They tried to embarrass me, they stole my boyfriends, they spray-painted bad things about me on the driveway, and they played as many tricks as they could on me, as if they could ultimately scare me off. Even my friends were my enemies at times. It seemed like every girl I knew was mean or had the ability to be mean at the drop of a hat.

10

Mean Girls made my life miserable for many, many years. But once I changed my focus and started looking to God instead of my meanies, things started getting so much better. I hope that this Bible study helps you be free of mean like it has helped me.

Your Mean

Mean Girls are everywhere, and if you are reading this book, then you probably know one very, very well. She might be your archenemy or your best friend, or she might even be you. But no matter who she is, it's time to stop the cycle of mean. I hope you've read the book *Mean Girls: Facing Your Beauty Turned Beast* and seen the light at the end of the tunnel. But now it's time to get down and dirty—yep, it's time to dig into God's Word and find all the gory details of his extreme love for you as well as his sometimes radical instructions on how "thou shalt live." Don't worry, I'm not going to get all old King James on you or anything. I just like throwing in a little old-timey flavor here and there. So if thou arest ready, shallest we begin?

Our Mean

When did it start, this mean of ours? Have girls always been catty and conniving? Was there ever a time when they cared for each other, looked out for each other, and actually liked each other? Let's take a look. Let's go back, way back to biblical times. A time before cliques and clashes. A time when mean hadn't fully hatched. Whether it was from lack of time or lack of the Internet, I cannot say, but mean simply wasn't.

Go back with me now to a time when each morning the guys would all leave at the break of dawn to work hard in the fields or the barns or ye old sword factory. And the womenfolk were left behind with the babies to do things like clean the clothes down at the river, pluck the chickens, make the bread, carry the water, and other girly stuff like that. It might seem so last millenium, but think about it for a minute. Imagine them all coming out of their grass huts or tents each morning and smiling at each other. They all knew each other like sisters because they spent every

MEAN >:|

doodle the face of mean in your life.

doodle the face of nice in your life.

Nice

waking hour together. They worked in community to do the things that needed to be done each day in order to live. Each woman worked hard on her tasks, cared for the community, chatted with the other girls, and lived her days with a common bond with all the other girls. In those days it wasn't every woman for herself. It was all for one. Each one did what they could to help the others. They didn't wake up in the morning and fight traffic to get to a dead-end job in an isolated cubicle, popping out only to meet another girl by the water cooler to talk about so-and-so and her big morning zit. No, there were more important things at stake, like, uh, survival. Without the community of women (and men), you didn't eat.

Now our mean has come to be an accessory to girl power. Our mean has become a survival tool for all the isolated and scared girls who lack love and community. And our mean has become our downfall. Instead of having around us a sisterhood of loving and caring girls, there to help us anytime we need them, we have made each other our archenemies. I cannot talk to a group of girls without hearing about mean. My estimate is that 99 percent of girls have some sort of Mean Girl in their life. Yep, 99 percent! What have we done? The very people made just like us—with the same emotions, hormones, and bad hair days—are no longer our confidants and refuge but are now our adversaries in the game of life.

How does that make you feel? Do you wish you had a group of girls who loved you and would do anything for you? Do you miss sisterhood? Do you want to stop the mean and start up the love? Well, then you've come to the right place. It might have to happen one girl a time, but it has to happen. We have to turn the tide of mean around and help girls like us find other girls who want more out of life. Our mean can be put to sleep, never to wake again, if we can one by one refuse it sanctuary. If we can choose to take the "me" out of "mean," then we can start today to put an end to this cycle that plagues our gender. Are you ready? Up for the challenge? Then let's grab hands and go, sister to sister!

What Do You Mean?

The purpose of this book is to help you stomp out mean. I know for a fact that mean inhabits all of us. And even if your mean isn't as bad as someone else's, the place you always have to start when it comes to changing the world is changing yourself. The first step in doing that is picking up this study. So nice job. Now the next step is doing the work within. Our mean can no longer be hidden. We have to get it out into the open where we can hose it off and expose it for the sin that it is. What do you mean, you ask? How are we supposed to do that?

First let's start with some ground rules. These aren't just rules for this study but should be rules for life, because they come out of the pages of God's Word. If you want to know God's Word and make amazing changes in your life, then live out these principles today and every day that's called today.

What This Study Is

1. This is a Bible study. Kind of a no-brainer, I know. But I want to make it clear that the purpose of this book is to study the Bible. Why? Well, because the Bible will give you the answers to who and why. Who loves me and will never ever leave me? Why do the things that happen to me happen? Why am I alive? Who is in charge of this crazy world? Who am I? And why do I do what I do? When you study the Bible you find the answers to those big life questions. And when it comes to Mean Girls, the Bible is your best escape. It's the most powerful weapon you can get your hands on. It can soothe you, help you, and heal you. If you are willing to risk believing that the words found in it are true and useful for even the meanest of girls, then you will soon find the peace you are looking for. So that's why this is a Bible study.

2. This study is about God. Again, no-brainer, you say? Well, you'd be right, but humor me. This study is about God. Who he is. What he loves. What he hates. Who he loves. How he wants what's best for you. How he will help you achieve that. How he works in your life. And most of all, what he wants from you. God. God. God. This book is all about God. The more you can make it about God and the less about this crazy world, the more you will get from it. Make sense?

3. This book is about you. But wait, there's more. This book is not only about God but also about you. It's about how you are living, what you are doing, and how that affects your relationship with God. It's going to grill you on the state of your soul, your thoughts, and your heart. It's going to help you dive into your motivations, your aspirations, and your disappointments. And best of all, it's going to help you learn to handle the Mean Girls in your life. I hope you're ready to open up and spill it, because that's what's coming up!

What This Study Is Not

1. This is not therapy. I know I said this book is about you, and it is, but it's about you in a healthy kind of non–self-absorbed way. It's not about you in a "*oh, woe is me, I'm the victim*" kind of way. It's not a place for you to vent your feelings and to be heard so that you can feel better. I know that sounds like tons of fun, but it's not the purpose of this book. Besides, there are people who get paid big money for that job, and I don't want to steal all their business. So let's leave therapy to the therapists. Like I said, this is a Bible study, and frankly, even if you feel right now that you need therapy to talk about your Mean Girl problems, I'm gonna bet that by the end of this book, there will be one less visitor to the therapist.

The purpose of this study is to teach you God's Word, and laying his Word onto your life and your heart gives the best healing you will ever find. This means no talking about, crying about, or complaining about the Mean Girl in your life. Eeek! What's that, you say? Sorry. Hope I didn't dash your dreams. But stop the freak-out, 'cuz what we are going to talk about is you! Now, that's not so bad, huh? Because you, after all, are the person **you** are responsible for. Since you cannot change anyone but yourself, you're going to need to turn your attention away from your Mean Girl and onto yourself. Any whining about her is futile and only makes the agony linger. It's up to *you* to understand God's Word for yourself and learn to live it. You can share what you know with other people, but you can never force others to be good or nice to you. You can never change others (i.e., the Mean Girl); only God can do that. And the best way to help bring that change that God will make in others' lives is to pray for them. Not about them, but *for* them and their relationship with God.

God gives you trials in your life to test you, not to allow you to whine and complain. So you will notice something in the questions you find here: they are all about *you* and not about what other girls have done to you. Like I said, this is not therapy. I'm going to ask you to be honest about yourself, your sin, and your mistakes. If you want the mean in your life to change, then that change has to happen in your heart. You'll understand this concept more as we move on. For the time being, just get your mind around the fact that this isn't the time to complain about your life or the girls in it. Think on this verse to get you centered:

Do everything without complaining or arguing, so that you may become blameless and pure, children of God without fault in a crooked and depraved generation, in which you shine like stars in the universe.

Philippians 2:14–15

2. This is not permission to gossip. Gossip is one of the favorite tools of a Mean Girl. So how hypocritical would you be if, while doing a Bible study on Mean Girls, you gossiped about a Mean Girl? Ironic, wouldn't it be? But it happens. No matter how bad someone is, if you are talking bad about them, you are sinning. Gossip is not allowed in this study. It's not allowed at all in the life of a believer. It is a silent killer. It tears at the hearts of girls all over the world. It drives them to depression, isolation, and even suicide. So let's not play around with such an evil weapon. The world has made gossip a tasty morsel to be bought at newsstands and talked about on the evening news, but it's not a tool in the arsenal of love. It's not for you. So don't allow it here.

He who covers over an offense promotes love, but whoever repeats the matter separates close friends.

Proverbs 17:9

3. This is not a time to hide truth. No lying to yourself about yourself, or about anyone else for that matter. This study will not work if you aren't willing to stop the lies and dig up the truth about yourself and your past. Being honest about the junk you've done is called confession, and it's the path to forgiveness. God's Word says, "If we confess our sins, he is faithful and will forgive us our sins" (1 John 1:9) and "all have sinned and fallen short of the glory of God" (Rom. 3:23). So the truth is, we've all been mean at some point in our lives, and we all need to come clean. Maybe you're the sweetest thing on earth and would never hurt another girl, but what about your thoughts? Have you fantasized about getting revenge? Have you dreamt of the day when they would get theirs? Those thoughts might not be destructive in your eyes, but in God's eyes it's the same as having done them. Jesus explained it like this: "anyone who looks at a woman lustfully has already committed adultery with her in his heart." (Matt. 5:28). If you dream of being mean, then it's time to confess and stop the thoughts that convict you in the eyes of God. Imagine a sisterhood where we all were so obedient to God's Word that we kept ourselves from even thinking bad thoughts about other girls. Mean would be gone. It wouldn't survive. And that is the call of God's Word. We have to be honest with ourselves and refuse to let even a small sin into our heart. So keep the truth in the front of your thoughts as we walk through this study.

Okay, I think that about covers it. Whether you're an underground Mean Girl or a famous one, you will have some work to do as you read this book. So be honest with yourself and your crew. And that means that whatever gets said here, stays here. If word starts to spread of the things said in this group, then mean has spread its evil grasp even further. Telling other people, even your bff, what was said in this group is gossip, and gossip is a tool of mean, not to mention a sin. So zip your lips! Can we all agree to that?

Let's say it together:

This is a safe place for everyone.

I will not gossip.

I agree that what's said here stays here.

Remember, this isn't a chance for you to be heard but a chance for you to hear God. So when you talk, talk from the perspective of what God is showing you or teaching you. Encourage one another, seek to become more obedient to God's Word, and most of all love on each other so that the power of mean will be thwarted!

Taking a Look in the Mirror

Now it's time for a little Q and A. Though this section is called Taking a Look in the Mirror, it's not just about you, it's also about looking at your gender more closely. Look in the mirror at yourself and all of us female types and get honest about us. The best place to start is with the current state of events. Let's get together and talk about why we do what we do.

Okay, here are the Qs to get things started:

1. Why do you think girls are mean to each other?

2. Why do you think guys usually aren't so mean?

3. When guys have a problem with each other, what do they do?

4. When girls have a problem with each other, what do they do?

5. How many Mean Girls do you know?

6. Do you have more guy friends than girlfriends? ☐ Yes ☐ No
   If yes, then why do you think that is?

7. Describe the perfect friend.

8. What is the biggest area of conflict for girls?

9. What's the meanest thing you've ever done?

10. Why did you do it?

11. How do you feel about what you did?

12. What do you want to get out of this book?

Now that you've spent some time thinking about the mean in your own life and how you want to change that mean—around you and within yourself—you're ready to really get started. As we go on we'll be digging more into God's Word and finding out the quickest way to eliminate mean.

So What's It All Mean?

We are all in this together, my dear ones. We are going to have some wake-up calls, and we are going to have some shocks to the system, but everything that strips away the old you and allows you to move more and more into the likeness of Christ is moving you a step closer to your destiny. Keep this truth in mind as you get ready for the next step in driving the mean out of your life:

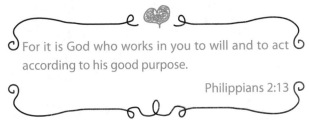

For it is God who works in you to will and to act according to his good purpose.

Philippians 2:13

Week Two

What's
Mean?

What's mean?

Think about it. Mean comes in all different kinds of packages. It can be totally obvious or totally subtle. In fact, a lot of times you might be doing something mean without even knowing it. That's why it's important to start off this study with a good understanding of what mean is. If you do a quick search in your Bible software or good old-fashioned concordance for the word **mean**, you aren't going to find the mean we are talking about. The only use of mean in the Bible is the one that has to do with "meaning" something—"That's not what I meant," stuff like that. **Mean** isn't a word that we can do a word study on, but we all know a little bit about the topic, so maybe we can put our heads together and come up with our own definition of mean. And from there we can look into God's Word and see what it has to say about the characteristics of a Mean Girl.

The Meaning of Mean

Webster's dictionary says, "mean suggests having such repellent characteristics as small-mindedness, ill temper." But that doesn't really seem to nail it, does it? So let's say *you* give it a shot.

1. What is your definition of mean?

   Mean = _____

   _____

2. What are some mean things people do?

3. Now look at your list and circle each mean thing that you also think is a sin.

4. What did you *not* circle?

5. Can you be mean and not sin? ☐ Yes ☐ No

Now that you've had time to think about what mean means to you, keep that in mind while we dive deeper into the subject of mean.

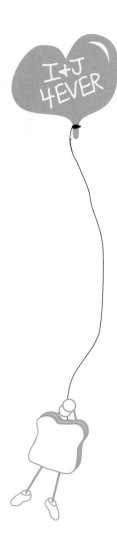

Find the Mean

Izzy loved Jack with all her heart. He was her dream come true. He was not only the cutest guy in school but also the nicest. He always spent tons of time with her, even when she was with all her friends. He liked going to the mall and hanging out. He loved chick flicks. He was just Mr. McDreamy. But one day all that perfection came crashing down, and Izzy was a wreck. She had thought they would be together forever, but she was wrong. And now Jack was gone. Moved on.

He broke up with her on a Friday night at the park. They were on the swings, just looking up at the moon and kicking their feet in unison. He said, "Izzy, I have something to tell you." He looked down at the dirt and cleared his throat. She smiled and said, "Yeah? What?" He looked at her with his steely blue eyes and said, "I can't date you anymore." Izzy put her foot down on the dirt and stood up in her swing. "What? What are you talking about, Jack?" she said. He said, "I just don't love you, and it's not fair to be with you anymore."

That's all she remembers of that night. She cried her eyes out for two weeks and then stopped. Now it's been six months and she still hasn't dated. But she is crying all over again. Why? Because her friend Jenna has been seen flirting with Jack. They aren't dating or anything, but they are obviously thinking about it, and Izzy's stomach is turning. How could she? Jenna knew how much Izzy loved Jack—how could she take him away from her?

Izzy went to talk to Jenna, and she said, "Yeah, I really like him, Izzy. And he really likes me. And since you broke up like six months ago, I thought it was no big deal." Izzy freaked out at that last sentence and told Jenna there was no way she would let her date Jack. She told her she had to stop liking him and that was that—or Izzy wouldn't be Jenna's friend anymore.

1. Who was mean in this story—Izzy or Jenna?

2. What did she do that was mean?

3. Why do you consider that to be mean?

4. Did Izzy have a right to tell Jenna what to do?

5. Is fighting over boys a sin?

> The girl who is **mean** for a reason is **still mean.** No matter what someone else does to you, it's **never an excuse to be mean back.**

Your first instinct might be to say that what Jenna did was mean. I mean, she had no right to date Jack. But is that really true? Does Izzy own Jack? The truth is that nobody owns anybody and the only person you can control is yourself. Since God calls us to love everyone, even our enemies, being mad at or mean to a girl who is dating your ex is ungodly and makes you the mean girl. Or should I say Izzy. Hopefully you can see from this story that the girl who is mean for a reason is still mean. No matter what someone else does to you, it's never an excuse to be mean back.

When Being Mean Is Being Nice

Arguably, the part of **American Idol** people talk about the most is the auditions. It's incredible how many people get up there to sing and are so unbelievably awful but think they are amazing. When the judges tell them how bad they were, some of them get so mad. They say things like "You don't know what you're talking about. My friends say I have an amazing voice," and "My mom thinks I'm the best singer in the world—you just don't know great when you hear it," and other crazy stuff like that. They can be so incredibly bad that you shake your head in amazement, but they just don't see it.

What happened? Are they deaf? Can they not hear themselves? And what about these people who tell them they are good? What's up with them? Are they just being cruel? Or do they think they are being nice? Some believe it's actually good to tell someone who wants to sing for a living, or in front of other people, that they just don't have a good voice. They, like Simon, believe they are just helping people to get closer to their real talent, whatever that might be. But what do you think?

Awesome!

You're Amazing!

Wow!

Incredible!

Wonderful!

Impressive!

Fantastic!

Umm...

1. Is telling someone the truth that they don't want to hear *always* mean?

2. Do you prefer to avoid the truth if it means hurting someone's feelings?

3. If what you want to say won't help the person and will only hurt them do you think it's a good idea to say it anyway?

4. Can you say something out of love and still have someone think you are mean? Will that stop you?

5. What does the truth have to do with mean?

> "Let us not become conceited, or irritate
> one another, or be jealous of one another"
> (NLT).

Week 2

1. What three things does this verse say not to
   do?

2. How do you think that telling someone the
   truth could irritate them?

3. How might reading this affect the way you
   tell them what you need to tell them?

do you
know it's
fact?

is it
helpful?

Read Galatians 6:1

"Dear brothers and sisters, if another Christian is overcome by some sin, you who are godly should gently and humbly help that person back onto the right path" (NLT).

1. How does this verse speak to 'keeping it real' with someone? i.e, when you feel like you need to tell them a truth that might hurt them?

2. How does it say you should confront people?

Sometimes honesty is not always the best policy. If you are saying something truthful but you are saying it just to hurt someone or make them feel bad, then you are being mean. If you are saying something truthful to help someone do better, be happier, or be more successful, then it might not be mean.

If you are saying something true only to make yourself feel better, and it might hurt someone, then you are being mean.

Mean Is as Mean Does?

Okay, so we've taken a little gander at what mean is and when being mean is actually being nice, and now it's time to step into the world of Mean Girls. Putting aside the nice motives of the "mean" we just talked about, let's look at the not-so-nice side of Mean. Think about some of the things people have done to you in the past or that you've seen done or even done yourself, and then answer these questions:

1. Without naming names, list some things people have done to you that you thought were mean.

2. Can you look up a verse that would support the argument that this Mean Girl act was a sin? If God isn't calling what she did bad, then do you think that getting upset over it is godly?

3. Here are some actions for you to judge for yourself. Which of these would you consider mean if they happened to you?

- Another girl flirts with your boyfriend, knowing full well you two are dating. Mean?
  ☐ Yes ☐ No

- Your best friend suddenly doesn't want anything to do with you. She avoids you every time you see her. Mean? ☐ Yes ☐ No

- A girl at school gives you dirty looks every time you walk by her. Mean? ☐ Yes ☐ No

- Your teacher gives you bad grades even though you know you deserve better. Is she out to get you or what? Mean? ☐ Yes ☐ No

- Your friend has a party and doesn't invite you. Mean? ☐ Yes ☐ No

Let me help you out and say that none of these things are sinful. None of these examples I gave are sins in and of themselves. It's not a sin to like someone else's boyfriend. It's not a sin **not** to invite someone to something. It's not a sin to give someone dirty looks. But are they mean? Hard to say. The trouble with all of these is that we can't judge the motives of the people doing them. You have no way of knowing what the girl giving the dirty looks is thinking, so you have no way of knowing if she is sinning in her heart or not. And it's not a sin to avoid someone or not invite them somewhere. Are you getting the picture? Girls can do some things to you that can feel awful, depending on how you think about them. And when you feel awful, you then label her actions as mean. And from there all kinds of thoughts happen—thoughts of revenge, hatred, fear, the list goes on. Before you know it, you're a Mean Girl yourself.

There will always be times in your life when people do things that hurt you. You will never get away from it. People hurt other people, but not all hurt is on purpose, not all of it is mean, and not all of it is sinful. If you can try to concentrate only on true sin—things that are truly mean—then you can forget things like someone not liking your dress or taking your boyfriend. If God isn't condemning what they did as sin, then why are you condemning them? The truth is that we are called to let things like that slide off our backs like water off a duck. Even when a girl seems mean, if you want to be happy and peaceful, then concentrate on not being mean in return. Getting revenge by hating her, slamming her, lying about her, or doing any other sinful behavior will not make you happy. It will make you mean.

Duck

Read Ephesians 4:31-32

"Get rid of all bitterness, rage and anger, brawling and slander, along with every form of malice. Be kind and compassionate to one another, forgiving each other, just as in Christ God forgave you."

1. God's word applies to even the victims of Mean Girls. What does this verse say that you should not do when a girl is mean to you?

2. What should you do, according to this verse, instead of getting her back?

3. Why?

Read Psalm 39:1

"I said to myself, 'I will watch what I do and not sin in what I say. I will curb my tongue when the ungodly are around me.'"

1. What sin is the psalmist talking about?

2. Is it harder to control your tongue when the people around you are nice or mean?

3. Why do you think words are so important that God repeatedly tells us to be careful how we speak?

The best thing to do is to do as the Bible says and rid yourself of sinful thoughts and actions. You can only change yourself; you can only take the mean out of your own heart. And that's the best place to start. When you really understand what mean is, you can find strength in the fact that if God has called you to do something, then you can do it. You can avoid being mean. And if he has called others to something and they are disobedient, he will deal with them. You just have to stay faithful and not take on the mean that is around you.

Make a list!

What kind things can you do for other girls this week?

So What's It All Mean?

We've tried to answer the question "What is mean?" But as you can see, mean can be tricky to define. Next time you feel offended, stop before you respond and take a look at yourself and into God's Word. Is what she did a sin? Or are you being overly sensitive and judgmental? Keep your eye on God and his law, and the mean in your life will most surely diminish.

"Stop judging others, and you will not be judged. For others will treat you as you treat them. Whatever measure you use in judging others, it will be used to measure how you are judged. And why worry about a speck in your friend's eye when you have a log in your own? How can you think of saying, 'Let me help you get rid of that speck in your eye,' when you can't see past the log in your own eye? Hypocrite! First get rid of the log from your own eye; then perhaps you will see well enough to deal with the speck in your friend's eye."

Matthew 7:1(NLT)

Week Three

Getting the
Mean
Out

So how did you do at defining mean in the last chapter?

Did you come to some consensus about what's mean and what's not? Figuring out what is mean is a tricky job. Each person might have a different take on it. And some nice things you say can be taken as mean by the person you say them to. So what's the deal—is there a good definition of mean? A good way to judge for yourself if what you are about to do or say is mean? Or is mean a moving target that changes with people's perspectives or emotions? That's the trouble with defining mean from a human perspective. Each of us is so different, and we can't possibly know what others are thinking or feeling, so knowing what each person considers mean is an impossibility. Thank God for ultimate truth. In God's Word we can find the ultimate answers about what we should and shouldn't do to one another.

The Sin List

The Bible is an instruction book that tells us how to live. It tells us about our God—what he loves and what he hates. As a believer you need to know both things. To better understand mean and how to remove it from your life, it's important to understand the things that God hates. Your hate list might just be a pet peeve list. In other words, a list of stuff that makes you crazy. But on God's hate list are things that are damaging not only to others but also to the soul of the person who does them. His hate list is a sin list. The things that God hates are things that not only are mean but should be off-limits to those who confess to follow Jesus. If we want to rid the world of mean, we have to get the mean out of ourselves first—we have to eliminate the things on God's Sin List from our lives. Let's take a look at Scripture and see what God says is too mean for his children. As we study these verses, add each sin that you identify to the Sin List on page 64.

47

> "Finally, all of you should be of one mind. Sympathize with each other. Love each other as brothers and sisters. Be tenderhearted, and keep a humble attitude. Don't repay evil for evil. Don't retaliate with insults when people insult you. Instead, pay them back with a blessing. That is what God has called you to do, and he will bless you for it."

1. Circle the word ***don't*** every time you see it, and then underline the rest of the sentence after it. Now read it again and double underline all the things you should do.

2. Have you ever said, "But she started it!"? When? Explain.

3. When someone else starts something and you do something back, what is that called?

   _____

4. Is revenge ever okay? Explain.

5. In the "Sin List" box on page 64, write one word that would describe what this verse is telling you is a sin.

Read 1 Peter 2:1 (NLT)

"So get rid of all evil behavior. Be done with all deceit, hypocrisy, jealousy, and all unkind speech."

1. Circle all the things that God tells you to get rid of or be done with.

2. Write down three or four things you see in this verse that you think are mean.

3. If the words used in your Bible translation don't seem like words you would use, then translate them. What are the words you would use to describe the sins listed in this verse? Are any of them commonly found in the lives of girls?

4. Add these words to your Sin List on page 64.

BLAH BLAH BLAH
BLAH

Read Proverbs 20:19

"A gossip betrays a confidence; so avoid a man who talks too much."

1. Do you know any girls who talk too much?   □ Yes (no names, please!)   □ No

2. Why is talking too much something to be avoided?

3. Add the sin listed here to your Sin List.

The Truth about Gossip

Here's a way to tell if what you want to say is gossip or just being honest:

If what you are saying will make another person disliked, hated, or even just look bad, then don't say it.

If what you are saying isn't fact, then don't say it.

If you heard it but don't know for sure, then don't say it.

If you are complaining about someone, don't say it.

If you are sinning by talking about someone (i.e., worrying, lying, hating, complaining, judging, criticizing, fighting, being jealous, etc.), then don't say it.

Read Psalm 34:12–18

"Whoever of you loves life and desires to see many good days, keep your tongue from evil and your lips from speaking lies. Turn from evil and do good; seek peace and pursue it. The eyes of the LORD are on the righteous and his ears are attentive to their cry; the face of the LORD is against those who do evil, to cut off the memory of them from the earth. The righteous cry out, and the LORD hears them; he delivers them from all their troubles. The LORD is close to the brokenhearted and saves those who are crushed in spirit."

1. Underline everything here that the author is telling you to do if you love your life and want to see many good days. Now put an oval around each use of the word "eye" or "ear" and a box around each word or pronoun used for "God."

2. Who is against the people who don't do what this verse commands?

3. According to this verse, what can the lips be guilty of?

4. What are some of the benefits of obeying these commands?

5. Add this sin to your Sin List.

New shades!
long lasting effects!

Lies

Jealousy

Gossip

Read Galatians 5:19–21

"The acts of the sinful nature are obvious: sexual immorality, impurity and debauchery; idolatry and witchcraft; hatred, discord, jealousy, fits of rage, selfish ambition, dissensions, factions and envy; drunkenness, orgies, and the like. I warn you, as I did before, that those who live like this will not inherit the kingdom of God."

1. Circle all the things listed that are sinful.

2. Now list the sins that seem to be the favorite of Mean Girls.

3. Is being in a fight (not just the physical kind, but verbal and emotional kind) one of these sins?

4. Is any fighting ever permissible?

5. Do you consider fighting, either physically or verbally, someone who has hurt you or hates you to be mean?

6. Add these sins to your Sin List.

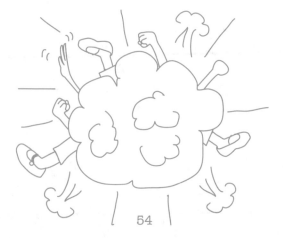

Read Romans 2:1

"You, therefore, have no excuse, you who pass judgment on someone else, for at whatever point you judge the other, you are condemning yourself, because you who pass judgment do the same things."

1. What do you think Paul means by this statement? How are those who do this condemning themselves?

2. What are some ways that you might judge another girl?

3. Have you ever criticized someone? Do you think this verse applies to criticism?

4. Add the sins you find in this verse to your Sin List.

Read Ephesians 5:5 (ESV)

"For you may be sure of this, that everyone who is sexually immoral or impure, or who is covetous (that is, an idolater), has no inheritance in the kingdom of Christ and God."

1. Circle all the sins in this list.

2. Look up the definition of **covet** and write it here.

3. What's another word for coveting that a lot of girls deal with?

   _____

4. Why do you think Ephesians says that coveting is idolatry?

5. What happens to people who covet what someone else has?

6. Is there anything that another girl has that you really, really want?

7. Do you think that it's a sin for you to want it? Talk about why or why not.

8. Add coveting to your Sin List.

Read Galatians 5:26

"Let us not become conceited, provoking and envying each other."

1. What does it mean to be conceited?

2. What two words does this verse use to describe the actions of a conceited person?

   _____

   _____

3. We usually think of conceited people as thinking they are better than other people, being super confident. But if they are really envious, then what do you think they are really feeling deep inside?

4. Add conceit to your Sin List.

Read Colossians 3:8

"But now you must rid yourselves of all such things as these: anger, rage, malice, slander, and filthy language from your lips."

1. Circle all the sins listed in this verse.

2. Which of them has to do with lying?

3. Does God consider lying a sin?
   ☐ Yes   ☐ No

4. The "But now" in this verse is in contrast to Colossians 3:5, which tells us to "put to death, therefore, whatever belongs to your earthly nature." Why do you think it's part of our earthly nature to lie about people?

5. The "therefore" in Colossians 3:5 is referring back to Colossians 3:1. Open your Bible and read Colossians 3:1–2. What are you being asked to do instead of the sins you circled earlier? (Hint: it is repeated in both the first and second verse. That means it's very important to get.)

6. Why are you being called to do that?

7. How can you do that?

8. Add all the sins you circled to your Sin List.

who turned out the lights?

Read 1 John 2:9

"Anyone who claims to be in the light but hates his brother is still in the darkness."

1. Circle the sin listed in this verse.

2. What does it mean to be in the darkness?

3. What does it mean to be in the light?

4. Add this sin to your Sin List.

By now you should have a pretty full Sin List letting you know what kinds of things God definitely hates. All these things can be considered mean. But what about those things that *feel* mean to you but aren't on this list? The question I want you think about is this:

why is your list of what's bad or wrong bigger than God's list?

Did God somehow miss a few things? Or do you think he covered all that needed to be covered? Beware of judging others' actions as sin if they're not on

The Sin List

God's list. Focus on getting the sin out of your own heart and life, and the mean around you will start to take care of itself.

Sin or Major Inconvenience

Creating the sin list was a good exercise, not only for finding out where you're maybe getting off track but also to find out how your mind's list lines up with God's list. If you find some things you think are mean that aren't on the list, don't assume they aren't sin, but don't jump to conclusions either. For example, if your best friend suddenly won't return your calls and is hanging out with other girls, don't jump to the conclusion that she is a horrible person. Is not returning your calls a sin? No. Then don't get all self-righteous and hurt.

If you look at everything that happens to you through the lens of God's Word, then you can start to loosen up over faux pas and uncool things that people do to you. When you get all riled up as if they are horrible people who have sinned against you, you essentially say that God's law isn't enough, that he missed a few things. That he should have added 'not returning my phone calls,' or 'not wanting to be my friend anymore,'

> **If you can lighten up about the things other girls do, you will find that mean has much less of a hold on you.**

or 'flirting with my boy-friend.' The list could go on and on. But should it? Don't you think that if God knew certain actions to be sinful he would have made them so? Now, this isn't an excuse for you to go out and be mean, steal boyfriends and ditch people you don't like anymore; you have to always live within God's law. And that means doing unto others as you want them to do to you. The point is that you can't judge the motives of the girls around you and the second that you do is the second that mean wins. Live your life according to God's law and trust him to deal with everyone else. If you can lighten up about the things other girls do, you will find that mean has much less of a hold on you.

So What's It All Mean?

Feelings lie. They can convince you of all kinds of crazy things. If you are feeling bad about another girl, stop. Take a look at your life and hers through the lens of God's Word. If there is sin, agree with God that it is bad and pray for the situation. But if there is no sin to speak of then stop talking, and stop worrying about it. You have enough things to occupy yourself with without getting all extra-biblical and making up your own sin list.

Understanding the things God hates is really an exercise for your soul. Take to heart what you've read here and trust that these truths, if believed in, will heal your life and your problems with mean. I know you want help with the Mean Girls in your life, but as I've said before you have to start with yourself before you can ever be free of others. Let this whole book be a lesson to you on how to live and how to be free from mean.

"Do to others as you would have them do to you. If you love those who love you, what credit is that to you? Even 'sinners' love those who love them. And if you do good to those who are good to you, what credit is that to you? Even 'sinners' do that. . . . But love your enemies, do good to them, and lend to them without expecting to get anything back. Then your reward will be great, and you will be sons of the Most High, because he is kind to the ungrateful and wicked. Be merciful, just as your Father is merciful."

Luke 6:31-36

Week Four

The Opposite of
Mean

Well, now that we've got a better understanding of what mean is, let's take a look at the opposite of mean.

If we are going to attempt to change girl culture, we need to really understand how to drop mean from our life. But anytime you take something away from your life, you have to replace it with something else, or that old thing just comes right back (Matthew 12:43-45). So if you're getting the mean out, what are you replacing it with? Let's dive in and figure it out.

What's the Opposite of Mean?

Before I tell you what I think, how about you take a shot at answering that yourself:

What would you say is the opposite of mean?

I think that most people would say that the opposite of mean is nice. Seems like a pretty good option, huh? But let me ask you this, just for fun: if I wrote a book called *Nice Girls*, would it sound like something you'd want to read? Are you really looking for ways to become a "nice girl"? Probably not on your top 10 list of goals. Sure, "nice" is nice enough, but it doesn't make much of an impact, does it? Don't get me wrong, I've got nothing against "nice." I'm nice. But when it comes to changing the world, I don't think that nice is good enough.

So what's the answer here? If God doesn't necessarily call you to be nice, what does he call you to be?

The answer becomes pretty clear when you look at God himself. What is the best description of God? According to 1 John 4:16, "**God is love.**"

Love

There it is. The opposite of mean: love. And it's more than what you might think. Love is more than a big red heart doodled on a notebook. It's more powerful than a good romance, more impactful than a dozen roses. Love changes people. It changes cultures, and it changes lives. Love is more than the opposite of mean; it's the opposite of all that is wrong with this world. And love can change this world.

But love is sorely misunderstood. We've kind of overused it, haven't we? We see it on bumper stickers and use it to talk about our favorite burger or TV show. And its true and powerful meaning has been lost. But have no fear, love is here! And it's more beautiful than ever. God's Word can lead us to an amazing if not mind blowing understanding of what love really is. So without further ado, let's have a look at love, God style!

God's Word Commands It

Love 'em or leave 'em. If you had two groups, the ones you loved and the ones you want to leave, which group would be bigger? God's Word says it better be the love 'em group, in fact, his words commands us to love all of 'em. Even the ones we'd rather never see again. Check it:

Read 1 John 4:8–12

"Whoever does not love does not know God, because God is love. This is how God showed his love among us: He sent his one and only Son into the world that we might live through him. This is love: not that we loved God, but that he loved us and sent his Son as an atoning sacrifice for our sins. Dear friends, since God so loved us, we also ought to love one another. No one has ever seen God; but if we love one another, God lives in us and his love is made complete in us."

1. Put a heart around every use of the word *love*. Then put a big triangle around the word *God* or any pronouns (*his, him, he*) used for his name.

2. If you do not love, then what does this verse say about you?

3. According to the end of this verse, what happens when we love one another?

"The commandments, 'Do not commit adultery,' 'Do not murder,' 'Do not steal,' 'Do not covet,' and whatever other commandment there may be, are summed up in this one rule: 'Love your neighbor as yourself.' Love does no harm to its neighbor. Therefore love is the fulfillment of the law."

1. What is this verse saying?

2. Why is love the fulfillment of the law?

God's Law

beard

Mt Sinai

After reading all of
these verses, you can see
that it's pretty clear that God
commands us to love. Loving others
is how we prove we love God and how we
prove that we are obedient. Without love, you
don't have God, because God is love. So if you are
a believer and you love God, then your entire life
will be colored by that fact. In your attempt to love on
God and show him your devotion, everything you do
will be done in the light of love. That means there's no
room for anything mean. There's no room for revenge
or hatred. You must love one another if you love God.
He commands it.

The Meaning of Love

Love. Seems like an awfully big word. God commands us to do it, but what in the world does "doing it" mean? What is the meaning of love? Let's take a look:

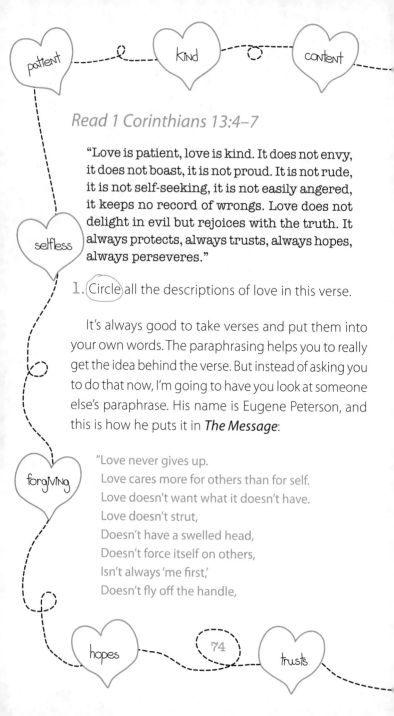

patient

kind

content

Read 1 Corinthians 13:4–7

"Love is patient, love is kind. It does not envy, it does not boast, it is not proud. It is not rude, it is not self-seeking, it is not easily angered, it keeps no record of wrongs. Love does not delight in evil but rejoices with the truth. It always protects, always trusts, always hopes, always perseveres."

selfless

1. Circle all the descriptions of love in this verse.

It's always good to take verses and put them into your own words. The paraphrasing helps you to really get the idea behind the verse. But instead of asking you to do that now, I'm going to have you look at someone else's paraphrase. His name is Eugene Peterson, and this is how he puts it in *The Message*:

forgiving

"Love never gives up.
   Love cares more for others than for self.
   Love doesn't want what it doesn't have.
   Love doesn't strut,
   Doesn't have a swelled head,
   Doesn't force itself on others,
   Isn't always 'me first,'
   Doesn't fly off the handle,

hopes

trusts

modest
humble
polite

Doesn't keep score of the sins of others,
Doesn't revel when others grovel,
Takes pleasure in the flowering of truth,
Puts up with anything,
Trusts God always,
Always looks for the best,
Never looks back,
But keeps going to the end."

coolheaded

2. What are your favorite parts of love after looking at this paraphrase? Why?

3. Which of these descriptions of love look like the opposite of mean?

Week 4

4. Have you ever been loved like this? Explain.

virtuous

5. So what is the meaning of love? Can you define it? Look it up in the dictionary if you have to. Then discuss.

protects

perseveres

6. After looking at this verse, can you think of anyone in your life that you love the way God commands you to?

7. Most everyone has trouble doing some of the things on this list. What are some of the things that you want to work on doing better?

After reading 1 Corinthians 13, you should have a better understanding of this love that God is commanding. The NIV version of this verse says that love is "kind." That might be where "love" is a good direct opposite of "mean"—when it is kind. But you could easily say that all the other descriptions of love are the opposite of mean as well. So the opposite of mean is something bigger than just being nice. It isn't about making people feel good or being agreeable; it's much, much more. It really is a condition of the heart and mind. It's an ability to let go of yourself and give, even when it hurts. To forgive, even when you don't want to. And to put others first, even when it seems impossible.

I know that this kind of love is a tall order. It isn't for the weak at heart. It isn't for the lazy or the wimpy. It takes hard work, and that work can leave you bruised

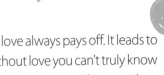

and aching, but in the end, love always pays off. It leads to peace and to hope, and without love you can't truly know God. If you want God to become more real to you, then you must understand love and offer it to everyone.

Love in Action

So now that you know you are commanded to love, how about we check out how the heck you are supposed to do that? I mean, love seems like such an elusive thing. Either you feel it or you don't. Right? Well, maybe not. Here's the thing: God commands you to love. But you and I both know that you can't command someone to feel something. I can't command you to feel sad or giddy right now. And if you've ever tried, you know you can't command someone to love you. So how can God command such an impossible thing?

Well, here's the twist: love isn't a feeling. It isn't about butterflies or chemistry; it's about action. God is commanding you not to feel but to act. And that makes it a whole lot easier. Still tough, but easier than forcing an emotion. You don't have to feel good about someone in order to love them—thank God! You have to choose to love in order for it to be so. So let's take a look at how love acts, and then we'll put our heads together to figure out how to make it happen.

Week 4

Love Isn't Concerned About Its Rights

Read Matthew 5:38–42

> "You have heard that it was said, 'Eye for eye, and tooth for tooth.' But I tell you, Do not resist an evil person. If someone strikes you on the right cheek, turn to him the other also. And if someone wants to sue you and take your tunic, let him have your cloak as well. If someone forces you to go one mile, go with him two miles. Give to the one who asks you, and do not turn away from the one who wants to borrow from you."

1. According to this verse, what should you do if someone takes your boyfriend?

2. Why would God ask you to turn the other cheek?

3. After reading this verse, does fighting for your rights seem like a holy act? □ Yes □ No

4. According to this verse, what rights do you have as a believer?

5. What would happen to girldom if every girl practiced this verse?

Love Is Obedience

Read 1 John 5:3

"This is love for God: to obey his commands."

1. Complete this sentence: Love is
   _____.

2. Can you explain how obedience can equal love?

3. Can people who don't truly love God ever love other people?

As you learn more about love, you might start to become more judgmental of those who don't love. But beware of judging others on this subject. Love isn't easy even for us believers, and it might just be impossible for nonbelievers. So don't be surprised when those who hate God also hate you. Never assume that you deserve more love and kindness from them than they offer to God. The best way to love those who hate you is to not take their feelings or actions personally. Remember, your goal is to imitate God. And God loved us all even when we hated him (Romans 5:8). Love is a bigger subject than we can cover in this little study, but as you start to grab ahold of some of it, do all you can to avoid losing any ground in your loving by being frustrated or angry with others who have yet to learn what love truly is.

Love Is for Mean Girls

So when it comes to love, who gets it? Of course you should love your family and your friends, but what about your enemies? What about those who hate you and hurt you? Do you have to love those people? It seems like a really stupid idea and maybe even a dangerous one. Loving those meanies can't be a good idea, can it? The answer is truly surprising. Loving the unlovable, the mean, is exactly who we are called to love. That's what makes us different from the rest of the world—those who only love people who love them back or can help them in some way. God's laws can seem like nonsense to those people. In fact, the rest of the world might even say that loving God's way is unhealthy for your self-esteem, but throw that craziness out the window and look at the truth.

A Journey through Mean

There's a great story in the Bible that really shows how powerful love can be when it isn't concerned about its rights. Joseph was a guy with a lot of mean going on around him. His brothers ganged up on him, the world seemed against him, but each mean thing that happened to him worked out for good. It's an amazing story and a good example of what obedience to God and his Word can do for all of us. So if you want to dig deeper and find out more about how to handle mean, get out your Bible and read the story of Joseph. It's found in the book of Genesis, chapters 37–50. As you read it, circle all the mean things people did and said to Joe. Then circle all the things Joseph did or said in return. Really look at how he handled mean. Then underline all the ways that he benefited from the mess mean people put him in. Underline all the amazing things that happened to him as he took his journey through mean.

Read Luke 6:32–36

"If you love those who love you, what credit is that to you? Even 'sinners' love those who love them. And if you do good to those who are good to you, what credit is that to you? Even 'sinners' do that. And if you lend to those from whom you expect repayment, what credit is that to you? Even 'sinners' lend to 'sinners,' expecting to be repaid in full. But love your enemies, do good to them, and lend to them without expecting to get anything back. Then your reward will be great, and you will be sons of the Most High, because he is kind to the ungrateful and wicked. Be merciful, just as your Father is merciful."

1. What is the payoff listed for loving your enemies?

2. Who are you imitating when you are kind to people who are mean?

3. According to Jesus, what should you expect in return from your enemies?

4. In the table below, make a list. On the left put the drawbacks of loving your Mean Girl. In the right side list the benefits of loving your enemies.

Drawbacks	Benefits

5. Are the rewards of loving your Mean Girl worth the trouble?

Read Matthew 5:43–48

"You have heard that it was said, 'Love your neighbor and hate your enemy.' But I tell you: Love your enemies and pray for those who persecute you, that you may be sons of your Father in heaven. He causes his sun to rise on the evil and the good, and sends rain on the righteous and the unrighteous. If you love those who love you, what reward will you get? Are not even the tax collectors doing that? And if you greet only your brothers, what are you doing more than others? Do not even pagans do that? Be perfect, therefore, as your heavenly Father is perfect."

1. What two things do these verses tell you to do for your enemies?

2. What do these pagans Jesus is talking about do that's so easy?

Love isn't just for your circle of friends and family. Although it is for them, it is also much, much bigger. The only way to prove your love for God and your obedience to his Word is by doing those things that go against your flesh, those things that make you freak out and say "no way." Doing those things not only proves your obedience but also changes your life from the inside out.

Think of it like this: the Mean Girl in your life—past, present, or future—might just be a gift from God which, if accepted and used correctly, can change your life and draw you closer to the one who loves you, God himself. To make that happen you have to stop the cycle of mean right here and now and shock the world around you by loving even those who are mean to you. It might not change their mean to nice, but it will change your heart and your mind and draw you more and more into the presence of God. Don't look for your payoff in the here and now. You might not see one until heaven, but either way, I promise you that the payoff will far outweigh the grief that you might have to go through in learning to love the mean people in your life.

So What's It All Mean?

God's love for you is perfect. It's the kind of love you dream of. And even if you can't feel it, I promise you God and his love are always present. Take some time today to notice all the things that happen in your life that point to divine intervention. What people has he put in your life that are drawing you closer to him? What books, thoughts, or dreams? When you concentrate on how much he loves you, it becomes a million times easier to love other people. His love is contagious, and because of that, you will be able to love even the ugliest of meanies.

And this is love: that we walk in obedience to his commands. As you have heard from the beginning, his command is that you walk in love.

2 John 6

Walking in His steps . . .

Week Five

Taking the
"Me"
Out of
"Mean"

So what do you think? Is love the answer?

Can love really fix the mean in your life? Love is an amazing thing. It's something we all really want and seldom really find, but it should be the goal of every believer. Unfortunately, we are human, and our humanness sometimes gets the better of us. I know from experience that it's super easy to throw love out the window when someone is mean to me. My first instinct is anything but loving. I get angry, I get hurt, I defend myself. I'm all over the place but nowhere near love. And every time I let a Mean Girl get the best of me by getting me to lose control and think stupid thoughts, I hate it. I think, what a fool am I? I know the truth, so why can't I just do what I want to do instead of doing the very thing that I hate? Being mean back to someone who is mean is the easiest and most comfortable thing to do.

Do you ever feel like that? Do you feel like people ought to be nice to you? Do you ever feel like everyone is out to get you? Or that a certain girl just wants to destroy you? It seems like there's always one. I know for me there were always many. I seemed to attract Mean Girls. Even today, when I walk into a group of women, I look around to see who's giving me the evil eye—only now once I find her, I don't run away from her; I run right toward her. I figure I'm not going to let her stinky personality affect my obedience and love. I go right up to her and become the nicest person she's ever met. It throws most of them off, and they usually warm up to me. It's funny how that works. Stop the mean by smothering it with love before it even gets started. Wow, maybe God does have something here.

Your life really has **little** to do with what **others are doing or feeling,** but it has **everything** to do with what **you are thinking and feeling.**

Remember, your life really has little to do with what others are doing or feeling, but it has everything to do with what you are thinking and feeling. If you want to change a situation, then all you really have to do is change your attitude. Change the way you think, and suddenly the world can get a lot more rosy. Being proactive and choosing love over mean is what will give you happiness and power. Power over mean: it's what can change girldom from a royal mess to an amazing thing. So now let's keep this show on the road and figure out just how to take the "me" out of "mean."

Your Mind, Your Feelings

Before we go any further, let's have a look into God's Word and see if we can't start making sense of the power of the mind.

Read Proverbs 23:7 (KJV)

"As he thinketh in his heart, so is he."

1. What do you think that means?

2. What do you think about the most?

3. What goes on in your mind when you meet a new group of girls?

4. What do you think when you meet a girl who seems mean or stuck up?

5. Are you sometimes scared of girls? Explain. What do you think girls will do that scares you?

Week 5

6. Write five words that you think apply to most all girls—not physical adjectives but things about their behavior or personalities. To get you started, here are five ways I might describe guys: physical, aggressive, in control, athletic, mechanical.

1.

2.

3.

4.

5.

Girls are . . .

Read Philippians 4:8–9

"Finally, brothers, whatever is true, whatever is noble, whatever is right, whatever is pure, whatever is lovely, whatever is admirable—if anything is excellent or praiseworthy—think about such things. Whatever you have learned or received or heard from me, or seen in me—put it into practice. And the God of peace will be with you."

1. Circle everything that Paul tells you to think about.

2. What is the reward when you do that?

3. Do the things you think about most fit into this list?

4. What kinds of things do you think about that don't fit into this list?

5. Why do you think that Paul felt it important to write this?

Week 5

Read Proverbs 4:23 (CEV)

"Carefully guard your thoughts because they are the source of true life."

1. What does this verse mean by "true source of life"?

2. What are some ways that you can guard your thoughts?

So what's all this talk about? Well, based on these verses, I believe that you are the sum total of your thoughts. Whatever you think about defines you. If you think about stealing all the time, then you're probably a thief. Think about God all the time, then I'll bet you're kinda godly—or getting there. Think about surfing? Are you a surfer? See, your thoughts are who you are. And your mind is where love gets its start.

If you are the result of your thoughts, then that means that the feelings you have are also a direct result of what you are thinking. It might seem ridiculous, but the Mean Girls around you really aren't what make your life miserable; it's **your thoughts** about those girls that can make you miserable. Your mind has the final say in your happiness. What you think will determine how you feel.

It's like this: sit down and watch your favorite tearjerker, and then tell me how you feel. Do you feel happy and uplifted? Or do you feel sad? Why? Nothing bad happened to you, so why would you feel sad? It's your thoughts' fault. Whatever you think about will affect your mood and your feelings. That means that if you think about how mean someone was or how unfair life is, then you're gonna be bummed. You get angrier and angrier the more you think about what someone has done to you. It's human nature. Any thought you insist upon thinking is going to grow into a feeling. You can't avoid it. So think about how wonderful your bf is and you're bound to feel giddy, butterfly-ey, and happy. It's not him making you feel good; it's your thoughts. Believe it or not, you can even make yourself sick based on what you think about. People have gotten things like ulcers, stomachaches, headaches, and all kinds of other ailments just by thinking negative things. The mind is a powerful thing. That's why God talks so much about it.

If you are what you think about, what have you been lately? Jealous and vindictive? Content and peaceful? Worried? Happy? Pay attention to your thoughts this week and journal about how they make you feel!

Week 5

When Mean Girls Make You Wanna Be Mean

A lot of times a normally nice girl can become a real meany just because of what some other girl has done to her. If you've ever said the words "but she started it," then you know what I'm talking about. It seems normal to stand up for yourself and even to fight back when being attacked, but the trouble is that doing that makes you a Mean Girl. I've said it before and I'll say it again: I believe that most of the problems that girls have with one another could be resolved if each one refused to fight back. If we all decided in our minds to think good thoughts instead of hateful, negative ones and if we all determined to control our minds and not allow sin to control us, then we could stop the cycle of mean before it could get its claws into you and the world around you.

The trick is learning to control your thoughts. You have to choose not to take the easy way out and think what the world wants you think. That kind of defeatist, victimized thinking is what can make your life miserable. If you can concentrate on God's Word and the truth in it, I promise you that the mean around you will lose all its venom. You might not get rid of the Mean Girl in front of you, but you can get rid of the "me" in mean.

Read Romans 8:6–8 (NCV)

"If people's thinking is controlled by the sinful self, there is death. But if their thinking is controlled by the Spirit, there is life and peace. When people's thinking is controlled by the sinful self, they are against God, because they refuse to obey God's law and really are not even able to obey God's law. Those people who are ruled by their sinful selves cannot please God."

1. What are some characteristics of your sinful nature that might control your mind? (Example: fear)

2. How do the two options for your mind that this verse describes relate to what we've just talked about?

Peace

Week 5

99

3. Can people whose minds are set on disobedience expect to find life and peace?

A Changed Mind

If you are having a hard time changing how you think and what you say and do, then dive a little deeper into the life of someone who changed everything in the blink of an eye. Paul was the ultimate meany—killing Christians, persecuting the church—but in one encounter with God he changed from a hater to a lover. He still struggled with his thoughts, but he learned to control them. His ability to renew his mind is my inspiration. See if it can't be yours. Read about Paul's past in Philippians 3:4–11; Paul's conversion in Acts 9:1–21; Paul's trials in 1 Corinthians 4:10–16, 2 Corinthians 6:3–10, and 2 Corinthians 11:23–30; and Paul's mind in Romans 7:7–8:17.

Read Romans 12:2 (NKJV)

"And do not be conformed to this world, but be transformed by the renewing of your mind, that you may prove what is that good and acceptable and perfect will of God."

1. According to this verse, what will change you?

2. What does it mean to "renew your mind"?

3. In what ways do you still "conform to this world"?

Week 5

Read Galatians 5:19–21 (NLT)

"When you follow the desires of your sinful nature, your lives will produce these evil results: sexual immorality, impure thoughts, eagerness for lustful pleasure, idolatry, participation in demonic activities, hostility, quarreling, jealousy, outbursts of anger, selfish ambition, divisions, the feeling that everyone is wrong except those in your own little group, envy, drunkenness, wild parties, and other kinds of sin. Let me tell you again, as I have before, that anyone living that sort of life will not inherit the Kingdom of God."

1. Circle the "evil results" listed in this verse.

2. Which of them seem like Mean Girl sins?

3. What does it mean to "follow the desires of your sinful nature"?

4. What happens to people "living that sort of life"?

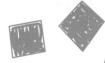

Read 1 Peter 2:23 (NLT)

"He [Jesus] did not retaliate when he was insulted, nor threaten revenge when he suffered. He left his case in the hands of God, who always judges fairly."

1. What did Jesus do when he was insulted?

2. What did he avoid doing when he suffered at the hands of those mean people?

3. According to this verse, what did Jesus believe about God (i.e., think) while he was being tortured?

4. What do you usually think about when you are being insulted?

Week 5

5. Have you ever been offended? □ Yes □ No

6. How does this verse apply to being offended?

Many times we are offended by what people say. It hurts our feelings or goes against our morality, and we get upset with them. When girls get mean, our first instinct is to protect ourselves, to fight for ourselves. But that instinct isn't godly; it's sinful. And it makes you into a Mean Girl. God understands your instinct better than you might think. While Jesus was here on earth, he faced bullies like you've never seen in your life. He was tortured, taunted, and ridiculed. But what do you suppose Jesus did when he was offended? According to the verse you just read, did he fight the offenders? Did he argue with them? No. Truth is that none of us should be offended by things said about us; we should be offended only by things said against God. Jesus never fought the offenses of others except when they offended God and made a marketplace out of his synagogue.

When girls **get mean,** our first instinct is to **protect** ourselves, to **fight** for ourselves. But that instinct isn't godly; **it's sinful.**

104

The life of Christ on earth is your example. He walked without being offended by what people said or did to him. Nothing anyone said against him mattered because he knew the truth. And the same should be true for you. Nothing any Mean Girl says about you can hurt you, unless you let it by taking it to heart. Try to stay out of the battle by refusing to become a part of it. Don't be offended when people hate you. It's to be expected—they are human, and because of that, they are messed up. But be vigilant for God. Stand up for the weak, stand up for truth, and stand up for his honor, but just keep yourself out of it.

To Fight or Not to Fight?

When it comes to Mean Girls, you always have two options, to fight or not to fight. Which will you choose from now on? Let's take a look at how we are told to react to mean:

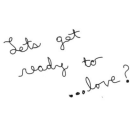

Lets get ready to ...love?

Read James 4:7

"Resist the devil, and he will flee from you."

1. What do you think this verse means?

2. How do you "resist the devil"?

A lot of people might use this verse to support fighting back or resisting Mean Girls. After all, if someone is doing something mean to you, then aren't they evil, and shouldn't you resist them? Interesting thought. But before I answer that, let's look at another verse.

Read Ephesians 6:12

"For our struggle is not against flesh and blood, but against the rulers, against the authorities, against the powers of this dark world and against the spiritual forces of evil in the heavenly realms."

1. Who are you really fighting against, according to this verse?

2. Who does that mean you are *not* fighting against?

"Then Jesus was led by the Spirit into the desert to be tempted by the devil. After fasting forty days and forty nights, he was hungry. The tempter came to him and said, 'If you are the Son of God, tell these stones to become bread.' Jesus answered, 'It is written: "Man does not live on bread alone, but on every word that comes from the mouth of God."' Then the devil took him to the holy city and had him stand on the highest point of the temple. 'If you are the Son of God,' he said, 'throw yourself down. For it is written: "He will command his angels concerning you, and they will lift you up in their hands, so that you will not strike your foot against a stone."' Jesus answered him, 'It is also written: "Do not put the Lord your God to the test."' Again, the devil took him to a very high mountain and showed him all the kingdoms of the world and their splendor. 'All this I will give you,' he said, 'if you will bow down and worship me.' Jesus said to him, 'Away from me, Satan! For it is written: "Worship the Lord your God, and serve him only."' Then the devil left him, and angels came and attended him."

1. How did Jesus fight the temptation that Satan was offering him?

2. What tools did Jesus use to fight Satan in this verse?

3. Based on this verse what are some ways you could fight the Mean Girl fight knowing what you already know about your thoughts?

After looking at Ephesians 6, you can get a better understanding of James 4:7. When you are told to "resist the devil," you are not being told to resist the Mean Girl. That would contradict the verses we looked at in the last chapter about turning the other cheek. Nope, what "resist the devil" is referring to is your thoughts. As we saw in Matthew 4, Jesus had to resist the devil when Satan made all his advances toward Jesus. But Jesus's resistance wasn't a fistfight; it was a mental battle. He heard Satan's warping of the truth and put the truth in his mind as his weapon of choice. Jesus had to choose to believe God's Word over Satan's words. And it's the same for you. You are called not to fight your Mean Girl but to fight your mean thoughts. Fight the lies that the enemy tries to put into your head. Because after all, God's Word makes it clear that your battle isn't against her; it's against the spiritual forces

of this world. She is just a person doing what people do—think about themselves. She's not your real enemy. Knowing the truth and using it to remind yourself and the enemy of God's Word is always your best defense in the battle of life. Focus on God's Word instead of her meanness, and you will immediately take the "me" out of mean and find peace instead of strife.

So What's It All Mean?

God's Word is really the only thing that will protect you from the world of mean. But it doesn't do it by itself, it does it by you reading it, learning it, and believing it. If you don't trust his Word, 100%, then you aren't going to get free from mean. You have to know that whatever happens to can be used for good if you are willing to believe that God can do it. Don't take the mean in your life as a life sentence—trust God's Word and make it a part of your everyday thought and you will be mean free!

Before we move on, let me leave you with these words of wisdom:

Rid yourself of all worry and pain, because the wonderful moments of youth quickly disappear. Keep your Creator in mind while you are young! In years to come, you will be burdened down with troubles and say, "I don't enjoy life anymore."

Ecclesiastes 11:10–12:1 (CEV)

Week 5

Week Six

No More Mean

Why do you think mean people are mean?
My mom used to tell me "they're just jealous." And that may be true, but more than likely those girls were just having fun. Human nature leads us to mean. That part of us that really wants to bond with others by gossiping, that part of us that wants so badly to be accepted that we do whatever we can to fit in—all those parts of us that long to be loved are the very parts of us that help make us mean. Any human who is untouched by the love of God is bound to find meanness a useful tool in the battle of life. It bonds like-minded people and it helps the mean person feel better.

But then there are us believers. We live not by the world's idea of right and wrong but by our God's idea. We believers know that what's natural to us isn't always what's best and that what's best isn't always that natural. And because of that, we struggle with mean. We can't understand why others hurt us. But any deep look inside will reveal that each of us has a human tendency to be mean. We all, I believe, at one point or another have done or said something to hurt another girl. You might hate it or you might not even know it, but either way, it's probably happened. But now that you know God's take on the whole mean thing, I hope you have a different attitude toward your own heart as well as the heart of the Mean Girl.

The Meaning of It All

Let's take a little look-see back and see if anything that you've read has stuck, shall we?

1. After doing this study, why do you now think that girls are mean to each other?

2. Are there some things you have done in the past that you *now* think were probably mean?

3. What's your definition of mean? (Has it changed from six weeks ago?)

4. Go back to Week 2 and look at your answers on #2. Do you still agree or have your ideas changed and why?

5. Can you be mean and not sin?   ☐ Yes   ☐ No
   Explain.

6. What do you plan to do the next time a Mean Girl starts something with you?

7. When it comes to other girls what is your weakness? In what area do you mess up the most? (Ex. Gossip, lying, envy, etc.)

8. Write down three verses that you can use as your weapons to fight against the pull to do something like that again.

9. What is the opposite of mean?

10. What are three characteristics of love, according to 1 Corinthians 13?

11. List three benefits of loving a Mean Girl.

12. Which is true for the believer? An eye for an eye or turn the other cheek? Explain.

13. What do you think is the most important thing that girls need to learn in order to stop the cycle of mean?

14. Do you know any girls who are fighting with a mean girl? What could you do to help be a peacekeeper?

15. What are some ways that you could help the girls at your school or youth group learn to get along better?

Before you go out and fix the world, think about your mission. How are you going to deal with Mean Girls now that you know what you know? Take a look back at some of the stuff you have written down in this book and let's get specific about how we can apply it in real life.

No Offense (from Week 5)

1. What did 1 Peter 2:23 say about what Jesus did when he was insulted?

2. The next time someone says something that offends you, how will you react?

3. What are some ways that you could lighten the situation?

Learn to Laugh

When someone makes fun of you, don't take it personal—laugh with them. It will shock them and it will help lighten the situation.

Don't let a joke at your expense ruin your day. Be humble and trust God to lift you up.

Remember, whatever they are saying about you or doing to you will never compare to what they did to Jesus. Are you better than him?

The Peacekeeper (from Week 3)

1. Look back at Psalm 34:12–18. When a MG starts her attack how can you be a peacekeeper?

2. What are some ways you could help your school be more peaceful when it comes to the girl population?

Making Peace

Do what you can to include all kinds of girls in activities.

Don't allow cliques to determine who you talk to or are friends with.

Remember that God loves even the MG and wants peace instead of anger.

Turning the Other Cheek (from Week 4)

1. How can you turn the other cheek when a girl is laughing at you?

2. What are some verses you can think about that will help you remember how to turn the other cheek and not be concerned about what she is saying?

Turning Fear into Love

Remember, it's not what happens to you but what you think about what happens to you that matters.

Say 'use this, Lord' or something like that, to yourself, every time a girl does something stupid.

Keep things in perspective. In the universe, this girl is just an itty bitty spot on a big huge earth, and in a matter of time she won't matter a lick in your life.

Loving Your Enemies (from Week 4)

1. In the next week what are two things you could do that would turn your anger into love for your enemies?

2. Write down five ways you can love your mean girl.

3. Talk to a friend who has a MG problem and share ideas on how to love your enemy together.

Lovers, Not fighters

Pray for her. Whenever you get mad or scared, just pray for her.

Ask God what he wants you to learn from this situation.

Spread the love. Look for opportunities to share the love to other girls around you, besides the MG. Make more friends, share love and spread good more than she spreads evil.

Week 6

I hope you have had a good discussion with your crew about these questions and the topic of mean in the eyes of God. Be sure to really dig in, get real, and don't be afraid to change. The more you change to reflect the will of God the more content and peaceful your life will be.

I told you in the beginning that I have had a lot of trouble with mean girls in my life. In fact, it's been most of my life. But, I'm happy to say, that isn't the case any more. After digging into God's Word and deciding to make it more important to me than anything anyone else could say or do to me I've been set free from Mean Girls. I don't have the stress or fear of Mean Girls any more. Did they all disappear or did I win them over to the light side? No. Wish I could say I had. I think they are still there, but I no longer look at them as mean, I look at them as hurting and I do what I can to brighten their cloudy days. I smile, I talk to them. And I live out God's Word. I've made some very good girlfriends along the way, and that has helped me to find a home where I don't have to seek the approval of the mean ones anymore.

I can't tell you how much better life is for me now that I've taken the power of mean away and given all the power to God. A few years ago a very bad thing happened to me at the hand of a kinda MG. She took away a dream of mine and I was shattered. It took awhile for me to get on my feet again and to see things from God's perspective, but when I did I finally saw that my life was

100 billion times better the way it was than the way I thought I wanted it. So for that mean moment I am thankful. Always look for the beauty in ugly moments. Look for God's hand reaching down through the black clouds. You will find it. But you have to believe! I did it, so I know you can too.

Changing the World One Girl at a Time

So could this be the end of mean in the world as we know it? Girls can be hurt by just about everything, so I don't expect girl wars to dry up completely. But if we could all agree to love no matter what, to forgive, to get over ourselves and refuse to retaliate, then the Mean Girl epidemic would dry up.

Are you willing to kill the mean and live the love? If you want to help yourself and the world of girls to draw closer to God, then now is your chance. You reading this book wasn't just an accident. You didn't stumble upon it on your own. There was some divine intervention. And now it's time to figure out why you have been chosen to heal girldom, because that is now your task. You can no longer plead ignorance and hide your head in the sand or in guyland. Whether you have been a Mean Girl, know a Mean Girl, or are the target of a Mean Girl, it's time to take action.

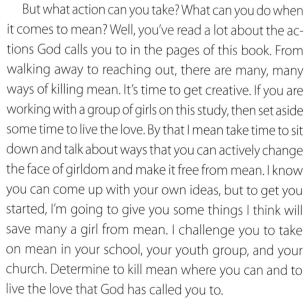

But what action can you take? What can you do when it comes to mean? Well, you've read a lot about the actions God calls you to in the pages of this book. From walking away to reaching out, there are many, many ways of killing mean. It's time to get creative. If you are working with a group of girls on this study, then set aside some time to live the love. By that I mean take time to sit down and talk about ways that you can actively change the face of girldom and make it free from mean. I know you can come up with your own ideas, but to get you started, I'm going to give you some things I think will save many a girl from mean. I challenge you to take on mean in your school, your youth group, and your church. Determine to kill mean where you can and to live the love that God has called you to.

I believe that if you and a few of your friends start to turn the tide of mean, you can and will save the hearts of many girls. You can teach girls to love each other and show them the God who makes this all possible. One of the best witnesses to the world would be groups of girls who love God and who love one another no matter what. So start today to redefine girldom. Give each other a break, forgive where forgiveness is needed, get over what needs to be gotten over, and remember above all that this world and all that goes on in it is not about you but about God and his plans. Take your eyes off of yourself and turn them upward. Reach out to those in need. Turn your cheek to those who hurt you, and do what you can to rid the world of mean.

Here are some ideas you can talk about amongst yourselves. They might seem hard, but remember, they are based in God's commandments, and therefore they are possible with him by your side.

The Shield—Find the girls who are the targets of Mean Girls and offer to shield them. Sit with them at lunch. Invite them to things. Give them a place to belong. Do things with them and for them. Even if they aren't believers, reach out to them. Stand in the way of the insults and attacks from others. Whisk them away from Mean Girls. Brag about them. Spread good rumors about them. Do all you can to brighten their lives.

Book It—Okay, you've done this book with a group of girls. Now each of you can break out on your own and find five more girls you can do this same study with. Also check out *Mean Girls: Facing Your Beauty Turned Beast*. It might be a good book for a book club you could start. Do whatever you can to get the conversation on this topic going. If you need to enlist the help of grown-ups, send them to the website nomoremean.com to find the leader's guide and ask them to walk with you and your friends through this study. Ask your moms,

your youth leaders, or whoever you know who has an ear for what you are talking about.

Get Techy—If you want to spread the news far and wide, then do an online campaign. Blog, chat, text—do whatever you can to tell other girls about your plan. Have them pick up the *Mean Girls* book or go to nomoremean.com to share your mean girl stories or your life as a former mean girl. Don't leave one stone unturned.

Talk to God—Start a prayer group with the sole focus of praying for girls. Make sure this doesn't ever become a gossip session. Just pray for their lives, their souls, their emotions, and whatever comes to mind. Start a revolution by going to the source himself.

Now it's your turn. Take this as a starter and find your own creative ways to get the mean out. Know that I am praying for you as you go. I can't wait to hear how it goes, so please fill me in on your progress. Add me as a friend at iFuse.com or ask me a question at askhayley.com and stay in touch with me about what's going on. I love to hear your stories! Thanks for daring to be different and to change the face of the world one girl at a time!

Your friend,
Hayley

Feed Yourself Some Truth
with PB&J!

The **P**ocket **B**ible Study **&** **J**ournal series includes studies on . . .

Dating
Mean
Hotness
Sex

Whether you're leading a peer group or an entire youth group, these pocket Bible studies and journals will give you everything you need to lead a biblical study on everyday issues like dating, relationships, modesty, and purity.

Also Available

Dateable: Are You? Are They?

Mean Girls: Facing Your Beauty Turned Beast

Sexy Girls: How Hot Is Too Hot?

Technical Virgin: How Far Is Too Far?

ℛ Revell
a division of Baker Publishing Group
www.revellbooks.com

Hungry Planet

www.hungryplanet.net

Leading a group through the PB&J series?

Here are some great resources to get your crew excited:

- **iFuse.com**: sign your group up in the new online social community from Hungry Planet!

- **HungryPlanet.tv**: download videos of Hayley introducing each section of the PB&J series

- **HungryPlanet.net**: download free leader's guides for the teen or youth leader

Need books for your entire crew?

For more information on church and youth group discounts, call: (800) 679-1957
Direct2Church@BakerPublishingGroup.com

Revell
a division of Baker Publishing Group
www.revellbooks.com

Hungry Planet
www.hungryplanet.net